Joke Books

by Judy A. Winter

Consulting Editor: Gail Saunders-Smith, PhD

CAPSTONE PRESS
a capstone imprint

Pebble Books are published by Capstone Press,
151 Good Counsel Drive, P.O. Box 669, Mankato, Minnesota 56002.
www.capstonepub.com

 Books published by Capstone Press are manufactured with paper
containing at least 10 percent post-consumer waste.

Library of Congress Cataloging-in-Publication Data
Winter, Judy A., 1952–
  Jokes about animals / by Judy A. Winter.
     p. cm. — (Pebble books. Joke books)
  Includes bibliographical references.
  Summary: "Simple text and photographs present jokes about animals"—Provided
by publisher.
  ISBN 978-1-4296-4466-2 (library binding)
  1. Animals—Juvenile humor. I. Title. II. Series.
  PN6231.A5W56 2011
  818'.602—dc22   2010002322

Editorial Credits
Gillia Olson, editor; Ted Williams, designer; Sarah Schuette, studio specialist;
    Marcy Morin, studio scheduler; Eric Manske, production specialist

Photo Credits
All photos by Capstone Studio: Karon Dubke except: Shutterstock: PeppPic, 20 (eye
patch), S.M., 16 (speakers), Sebastian Knight, cover, 14 (cow), trucic, background
(throughout), vladmark, 10 (city skyline)

Note to Parents and Teachers

The Pebble Jokes set supports English language arts standards related
to reading a wide range of print for personal fulfillment. Early readers
may need assistance to read some of the words and to use the Table of
Contents, Read More, and Internet Sites sections of this book.

Printed in the United States of America in North Mankato, Minnesota.
122010   006032R

Table of Contents

Cats, Dogs, and Fleas

What do cats eat for breakfast?

Mice Crispies.

What did the cat call the mouse on rollerblades?

A meal on wheels.

What is a kitten's favorite color?
Purr-ple.

What do you call it when a kitten stops?
A paws.

What kind of dog
likes to take baths?

A shampoodle.

What is a dog's
favorite dessert?

Pup-cakes.

What city do dogs like to visit?

New Yorkie.

Where should you never take your dog?

A flea market!

What do you call a pig that knows tae kwon do?

A pork chop.

What do you get when you cross a pig and a cactus?

A porky-pine.

What is a cow's favorite subject in school?

Moo-sic.

What do cows do on a Friday night?

They go to a moo-vie.

What is a rabbit's
favorite dance?

Hip-Hop.

Why was the
rabbit crying?

He was unhoppy.

What do you give
a sick bird?

A tweetment.

What do you get when
you cross a caterpillar
with a parrot?

A walkie-talkie.

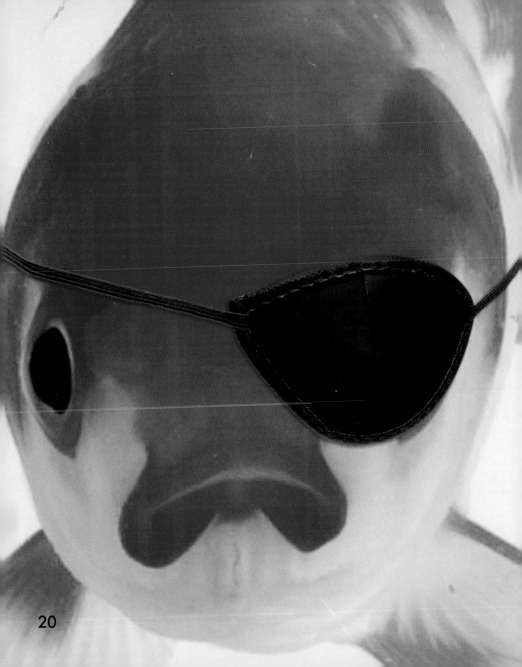

What do you call
a fish that doesn't
have an eye?

Fsh.

What do you get when you
cross a shark and a cow?

**I don't know, but you
wouldn't want to milk it!**

What do ducks like
to eat with soup?

Quackers.

What time of the day
does a duck wake up?

At the quack of dawn.

Read More

Charney, Steve. *Kids' Kookiest Riddles.* New York: Sterling, 2007.

Phillips, Bob. *The Awesome Book of Cat Humor.* Eugene, Ore.: Harvest House, 2009.

Ziegler, Mark. *Fur, Feathers, and Fun! A Book of Animal Jokes.* Read It! Joke Books—Supercharged. Minneapolis: Picture Window, 2006.

Internet Sites

FactHound offers a safe, fun way to find Internet sites related to this book. All of the sites on FactHound have been researched by our staff.

Here's all you do:

Visit *www.facthound.com*

Type in this code: 9781429644662

Word Count: 221   **Grade:** 1
Early-Intervention Level: 18